In Praise of Mermaids

A recipe book

Alison Murray

Published by All2Knit
High Rising
Northdown Road
Bideford
Devon
EX39 3LP

www.all2knit.co.uk

ISBN 978-0-9561715-1-1

(Front & Back cover pictures © Mike Lester)

Artwork & Print by B.A.P.S. Publishing Ltd, 01237 425178

In Praise of Mermaids

I grow old...I grow old...
I shall wear the bottoms of my trousers rolled.
Shall I part my hair behind? Do I dare to eat a peach?
I shall wear white flannel trousers, and walk upon the
beach.
I have heard the mermaids singing, each to each;
I do not think that they will sing for me.

The Love Song of J. Alfred Prufrock

T. S. Eliot

Like Prufrock, I have heard the mermaids singing.
A few years back my wife and I took the ferry across to
Lundy Island. We walked to the northern tip and snuggled
down amongst the rocks on the cliff top to eat our picnic. As
we ate our ears were assailed by an eerie but melodious
wailing that made our hearts tremble. Creeping to the edge
we peered over the cliff and there, on the beach below were
a number of grey seals hauled up amongst the rocks and
wailing their plaintiff song.

The singing of seals is one of the many suggested
sources for the legends of mermaids as are the more
unlikely dugong and manatee of the warmer waters of South
America. Whatever their true origins, tales of these iconic
spirits stretch far back in time and can be encountered far
and wide. Dagon, a fertility god of ancient Mesopotamia,
was half man and half fish, and the Ancient Greeks believed

the sea and ocean were peopled with tritons, nereids and oceanids. Tales are told in Scotland of the Silky of Sule Skerry and in Cornwall merrymaids all around the coastline while even in Oaxaca, in the heart of Mexico, you can hear the story of La Sirena, a girl who loved to wallow in the cool streams rather than carry out her chores only to awake one day with her legs transformed into a fishy tail.

The classic image of the mermaid with a looking glass in one hand and a comb in the other is well known and can be found carved onto the sixteenth century pew ends of churches in Cornwall such as Kilkhampton and, more famously, Zennor. She appears as a traditional motif on embroideries all across Europe and I even once spotted her on a piece of metalwork in Marrakesh.

She is the spirit of the waters and like them she is to be treated with respect. Although she may bring good luck she can also be the harbinger of storms. Several Westcountry harbours, like the one at Padstow in the Camel estuary, have a story relating to a merrymaid [the Cornish for mermaid] who protected the harbour, preventing its silting up, until one day she was treated disrespectfully and left in high dudgeon, leaving the harbour useless or in constant need of dredging.

The mermaid is a truly iconic image. What little girls has not at some time wished she was a mermaid? She has a powerful place in the collective unconscious. Why is that? If we stare out to sea long enough, if we listen hard enough, might we see her combing her hair, might we hear her singing?

Bryan Sentance

Contents

(All recipes included in this book have been included as given but we can accept no responsibility for any errors therein)

Introduction

In 2005 we began to organise a local community-knitting project to make the worlds largest knitted Christmas tree. Although this rapidly became a national project we are still amazed at the response we received for that and our subsequent projects.

The Christmas Tree was followed by the Giant Knitted Gingerbread House in 2006/7 and the response was even greater. Following its launch in Devon in the summer of 2007 it began its tour of the UK with the ICHF exhibition organization and travelled to Exeter, Harrogate, Brighton, Cardiff, Glasgow, Birmingham and Liverpool, which lasted until the spring of 2008.

Early in 2009 the Gingerbread House visited a major exhibition in Paris and then went on to Newcastle.

In September 2009 it went on a 4-week sea voyage to the Far East to be displayed for three weeks in Bangkok, Thailand, to support the launch of a Thai knitting charity event. It received great attention and attracted many knitters, both new and old, for their project called "Knit for The Needy".

Everywhere it toured we met more people wanting to be involved in one of our projects so we had to think of something new and as we live near the coast in Devon we began to think of a sea theme. The question was should it be something above or below the sea. Finally we decided it should be both and on this occasion we wanted people to experience something quite different so "Above and Below The Waves" was born.

The structure was to be a much bigger than The Gingerbread House and we wanted people to be able to go inside it so that they could experience being under the sea as well as seeing the coastline on the outside.

We started by contacting as many of our previous knitters together with all those who had volunteered their help when we toured. Magazines, web sites and newspaper articles all helped to spread the word. With the scope of our new project all our knitters had the chance to be even more creative and challenged. Soon we were receiving all sorts of sea life from coral to seaweed and fish, Puffins from Hong Kong, Punch & Judy from Coombe Martin, and many, many mermaids of all shapes and colours. Everything, right down to the smallest shell and pebble was carefully stored away for the construction.

We have been amazed and greatly impressed with all the variations and the quality of the knitting and crocheting we have received.

We also visited Bradworthy Junior School in Devon and The Steiner School in Bristol where we taught the children to knit and they were all keen to be involved with the project.

Countless parcels arrived throughout 2009 and by the start of 2010 we were getting ready for the construction phase of the project. On this occasion we decided to approach the Arts Council for a small grant towards the construction costs and in early 2010 we learnt we had been successful. We had also been asked to display the finished project at The Appledore Visual Arts Festival in June 2010 and this became our target. We had also been invited by ICHF to

again tour with them to their exhibitions.
We knew we would need a lot of space for the construction
and were lucky to be given the use a large hall at nearby
Kingsley School in Bideford, Devon.

The actual construction took around five months. There
were four or five of our local knitting group every day of
the week sewing the project together. We estimate that there
was around 2000 hours of sewing involved..

This project was technically more challenging, as it
involved a larger structure and also required interior
lighting.

Finally June 2010 came and we went to The Appledore
Visual Arts Festival. It was wonderful to watch people's
expressions as they came into the hall where the exhibit
was and as they began to look around they began to
discover all the little details. Everyone was greatly
impressed by the finished result.

Even the local Appledore Lifeboat Crew came along. I had
knitted a model of their new lifeboat, The Molly Hunt, a
brand new Tamar class boat, which had just come into
service with them.

We have since displayed "Above and Below The Waves" at
Kingsley School, Bideford and R.H.S. Rosemoor in Devon.

Our previous projects have raised over £40,000 for various
charities, mainly The North Devon Hospice and Great
Ormond Street Hospital for Sick Children.

On this occasion we will be collecting donations for the
R.N.L.I. while touring the UK as we are supporting their

"Train One to Save Many" national training campaign. All of our projects have given enormous enjoyment to all the knitters and helpers who have contributed and it is a credit to all their hard work that is has given such pleasure to the many thousand of people who have already seen the projects across the UK and will continue to do so at future exhibitions.

As with our previous book "In Praise of Ginger" we asked our knitters to send us their favourite recipes, this time, of a nautical nature, and we thank every one of you for your recipes. We hope there is something for everyone.

Thanks again to all the fantastic knitters, helpers and contributors without whom we could never have created these amazing knitted projects.

Alison and Ann Murray
September 2010

Shark attack

by Mike Jubb

The shadowy shape of a shark
Will make a dogfish bark,
Or make a catfish climb a tree in fright.
How the hake and haddock hustle,
While the cockle shows his mussel,
And the dace must find a plaice that's out of sight.

When the shark is on the gobble,
How the jelly-fish will wobble,
How the cuttle-fish will scuttle to its hole.
But the crayfish and the cod
Do the conger, which is odd;
And the ray can only pray to save its sole.

When the shark is being sharkish,
All the shellfish and the starfish
Hide the winkle in a twinkle from his jaws.
But the whiting will not wait
As the scallops try to skate,
And the sea-horse gallops off to hide indoors.

To avoid old sharky's gullet,
The mackerel and the mullet
Leave the roach and loach to flounder in the lurch.
But the tuna and the tuny
Can't see anyfin that's funny
When the flying fish falls laughing off its perch.

When the shark has had his fill,
And he's feeling rather brill,
How the herring and the halibut will sigh.
How the turbot and the trout
And the shad will give a shout;
But the crab will dab a teardrop from its eye.

Now the shark has finished fishing,
And the wrasse and bass are missing,
With the salmon and the sardine and the scat;
Let us find a fishy thought
For those clownfish that were caught:
I hope you won't be such a silly spratt !

Whitefish

Coastal Crumble

(A supper dish for two)

The title is a joke as the Naze, (a local beauty spot), is crumbling into the sea.

Ingredients:

A selection of seasonal vegetables, washed, chopped or sliced.
e,g, courgette, carrot, spring onion or leek, cauliflower or broccoli cut into small pieces.

400mls of white sauce, not too thick, seasoned with salt and pepper.

2 tablespoons of grated cheddar cheese

Crumble mix;- 50gms butter, rubbed into 100gms plain flour, add a heaped tablespoon of crushed cornflakes, salt and pepper and a teaspoon of mixed herbs.

Method

Put the prepared vegetables into a well buttered ovenproof dish. Cover with the sauce and then a spoonful of grated cheese. Sprinkle the crumble mix on top and press down gently. Put the rest of the cheese on top.
Bake at 180C for about 40 minutes, until top is brown.
As a main meal add some fresh cod cut into small pieces to the vegetables in the bottom of the dish.
To make a more nutritious vegetarian dish add some chopped cashew nuts to the crumble mix.

I make a gluten free version of this, using Doves Farm plain white flour and Mesa Sunrise flakes. I also use Doves Farm flour for the white sauce.

Tricia Tanti, Essex

Cod Baked In Cider

Ingredients

1lb cod fillet	Salt and pepper
2oz. mushrooms	2 tomatoes
Margarine	Cider
Grated cheese	

Method

Skin the fillets of cod and cut into pieces and place into a baking dish. Season. Cover with slices of mushroom and tomato and place small pieces of margarine all over.

Nearly cover with cider. Place greaseproof paper or foil on top and bake in a moderate 375 F for about 30 minutes.

Remove from the oven and make a sauce with a little fat and flour and the liquid. Season to taste and pour over the fish.

Sprinkle with grated cheese and garnish with slices of tomato. Return to the oven for 10-15 minutes to brown the top.

Creamed potato can be piped around the fish before returning to the oven if desired.

Jean Horncastle, Paignton

Cod in Spicy Tomato Sauce

Ingredients

4 cod steaks (approx 1 kilo)
14 oz tin chopped tomatoes
1$^{1}/_{2}$ tsp salt
$^{1}/_{4}$ tsp turmeric
1 tsp whole mustard seeds
2 tsp ground coriander - cumin
$^{1}/_{2}$ tsp ground roasted cumin seeds
2 tbsp creamed coconut

1 medium onion
9 tbsp cooking oil
1 tsp red chilli powder
1 tsp whole fennel seeds
2 tsp garlic paste
6 curry leaves
$^{1}/_{2}$ tsp garam masala

Method

Wash and dry fish. Rub with salt ($^{1}/_{2}$ tsp) and chilli powder ($^{1}/_{2}$ tsp) and turmeric ($^{1}/_{4}$ tsp). Set aside for 30 minutes.

Heat 4 tbsp of oil in frying pan (medium heat) when oil is hot add fennel and mustard seeds, after a few seconds add finely chopped onion and garlic paste, stir and fry until onions are slightly brown.

Add coriander-cumin powder, rest of salt and chilli powder. Stir and add tomatoes, curry leaves, ground roasted cumin seeds, coconut and garam masala. Bring to the boil then cover the pan and simmer for 15 minutes.

Heat the remaining oil, (5tbsp), in frying pan. When hot add fish steaks and brown quickly on both sides. Finally in order for fish to cook thoroughly add the spicy tomato sauce and cook for about 15minutes or until the fish is cooked through.

Alia Allim, Cardiff

Baked Coley with Lime Crust

(Meal for 1)

Ingredients

25g (1oz) fresh ciabatta breadcrumbs
1 tbsp fresh parsley, chopped finely
zest and juice of 1 lime
salt and ground black pepper, to taste
1 x170g (6oz) coley cutlet

Method

1. Preheat oven to 425deg F, 220 deg C, gas mark 7.
Grease a baking sheet very lightly.

2. Mix breadcrumbs with the parsley, lime zest and half the
juice. Season the mixture well.

3. Place fish on baking sheet and drizzle over remaining lime juice. Bake in
the oven for 10 minutes.

4. Remove from oven and press breadcrumb mixture down lightly over the
fish. Return to oven and bake for a further 15-20 minutes or until the
breadcrumbs are crisp and golden and the fish is completely cooked.

5. Serve with a fresh green salad and lemon wedges.

Ivy Voysey, Somerset

Fish Bake 1

Ingredients

1^1/$_2$ lbs potatoes cooked and diced
12ozs each of cod fillet and smoked haddock cubed
Mornay sauce   4 tbsp parsley chopped
25g butter   1 oz grated cheese
25g flour   1 pint of milk

Method

Place fish in ovenproof dish, make sauce and pour over fish. Top with potato and cheese.

Bake for 25 minutes at 200C gas mark 6

Garnish with parsley.

Mair, Lewis, Flintshire

Fish Bake 2

Ingredients

1lb grated potatoes   1^1/$_2$ cooked and flaked fish
salt and pepper   (cod, hake. Haddock, mackerel)
2 large grated onions ^{1}/$_4$ pint of milk
2 tbsp chopped parsley

Method

Grease a shallow casserole well. Put a layer of grated potato on the bottom, season well, add a sprinkling of onion and parsley then a layer of fish. Continue with these layers to fill the casserole, ending with a layer of potato. Pour over the milk. Cover with a piece of greased paper, put the on lid. Bake in the centre of a moderate.180C, 350F or Gas mark 4 for 30-35 minutes. May be served hot or cold.

Anne- Marie Caine, Exeter

Fish Cake with Chilli Cream

Ingredients

650 gms floury potatoes such as Maris Piper or King Edward peeled.
225gms shelled young broad beans
900gms firm white fish or salmon fillets
Plain flour for dusting
Olive oil for shallow frying
Crème fraiche and chilli sauce to serve

Method

1. Cook potatoes in boiling water for 20 minutes, adding the beans for the last 5 minutes. Meanwhile poach the fish in 600ml water in saucepan for 8-10 minutes until tender.

2. Drain the fish and cool slightly then flake into chunky pieces discarding skin and bones. Drain potatoes and beans and mash together. Fold the fish into the mixture and season, then shape into 8 patties and dust lightly with flour.

3. Cover bottom of non-stick frying with oil and heat until hot then fry fish cakes for 3-4 minutes on each side until golden brown.

4. Serve with a pot of crème fraiche and drizzle with chilli sauce.

Pat Hindson, N. Devon

Italian Baked Fish

Ingredients

4 thick slices of white fish
1 medium onion finely chopped
1 clove garlic crushed
14oz tin Italian tomatoes
1 tsp basil
2 tbsp olive oil
14oz mushrooms thinly sliced
1 dsp black olives
 juice of half a lemon
salt and pepper

Method

Pre-heat oven to gas mark 5, 375F, 190C
The Sauce: Heat olive oil in a saucepan and fry onion for 5 minutes, add
the garlic and tomatoes. Season with salt and pepper then stir in the basil.
Simmer gently uncovered for 15 minutes, stirring occasionally. Next add
mushrooms and stir in.
Simmer for 10 minutes until it looks like a thick puree. Place fish in a
shallow baking dish and sprinkle with lemon juice.
Next spoon puree onto each fish and arrange olives on top.
Cover with foil and bake for 25 minutes. Serve with rice or a tossed green
salad.

Absolutely delicious!

June Peace, Christchurch, Dorset

Oriental Fillets

Ingredients

Metric	Imperial
4x175g white fish fillets	4x6oz white fish fillets
Salt	Salt
freshly ground pepper	freshly ground pepper
2x15ml spoons oil	2 tbsp oil
50gms butter	2oz butter
1 garlic clove crushed	1 garlic clove crushed
12 thin slices fresh ginger	12 thin slices fresh ginger
or 1x5ml spoon ground ginger	or 1x tsp ground ginger
1x15ml spoon sugar	1 tbsp sugar
1x15ml spoon cider or	1tbsp cider or
Wine vinegar	wine vinegar
2x 15ml spoons soy sauce	2 tbsp soy sauce
3x 5ml spoons cornflour	3 tsp cornflour
5x 15 ml spoon water	5 tbsp water

To garnish 4 spring onions chopped, a few unpeeled prawns.

Cooking time 20 minutes

Method

Rinse and dry the fish, season with salt and pepper. Heat the oil and butter in a frying pan, add the fillets and fry until they flake easily, about 5 minutes on each side depending on the thickness. Arrange the fish on a hot serving dish and keep warm. Add the garlic and ginger to the fat in the pan. Mix the sugar, vinegar and soy sauce together and add to the pan. Mix the cornflour together with the water and stir into the mixture, stirring continuously over the heat until it thickens and is smooth. Pour over the fish, garnish with spring onions and prawns. Serve with fried rice.

Lindsay Norman, Hong Kong

Fish crumble

Ingredients

1 1/2 lbs cooked white fish flaked
3 hard-boiled eggs roughly chopped
4oz prawns (optional)

Crumble Mix
1 1/2 oz butter
3oz plain flour
2oz cheese (grated)
Salt and pepper

Béchamel Sauce
1 pint flavoured milk
1/2 oz plain flour
1/2 oz butter

Method

Set oven to 350F or Gas mark 4
To make the crumble, rub the butter and flour together add the remaining ingredients. Set the mixture aside.

Make the béchamel sauce.
Mix the fish with the chopped egg and prawns if used. Add to the béchamel sauce and turn into an ovenproof dish. Cover the mixture with the crumble topping and put in pre-set moderate oven for about 20-30 minutes to brown.

Jean Davie, Salcombe

Fish Dish

Ingredients

1/2 to 3/4 lb best haddock
A good knob butter

2 eggs
A little milk, salt and pepper

Method

Boil haddock until tender in water. Chop finely.
Add beaten egg, milk, butter and seasoning, and mix well.
Turn into an oven dish and bake in a moderate oven until set.

Jean Horncastle, Paignton

Fish and Lemon Pie

Ingredients

1 1/2 lbs hot mashed potato
1 lb cod fillet
2 onions sliced
2 carrots sliced
1/2 pint water
2 tbsp corn oil

1oz cornflour
Juice of 1 lemon
1/4 - 1/2 level tsp basil
1oz breadcrumbs
Parsley and lemon twists to garnish

Method

1. Pipe around the side of a 2pt dish with mashed potato.

2. Skin the fish, cut into cubes and boil with onions and carrots in approximately 1/4 pint of water for 15 minutes. Strain and make the stock up to 1/2 pint with water.

3. Heat the corn oil add the cornflour and mix the stock slowly and bring to the boil stirring all the time, cook for 1 minute.

4. Add the lemon juice, fish, vegetables and basil, mix well and pour into centre of pie dish.

5. Cover with breadcrumbs and bake in hot oven, Gas mark 7, 425F for 20 minutes, until top is browned. Garnish with parsley and lemon twists.

Ivy Voysey, Somerset

Fish Olives

5 oz fish per person (cod or haddock). Wrap in smoked salmon brush with a little oil and bake for 20- 25 minutes in a medium heat oven 150-140C

Meanwhile brown a chopped onion in a tsp of 'easy garlic' in oil and add a tin of tomatoes and a tsp of tomato puree and simmer until it is a thick sauce.

Serve with new small potatoes and green vegetables.

Janet Shanks, Crieff, Perthshire

Fish Shells

Makes 4 servings

A very tasty dinner party starter, as they can be made in advance, and frozen without the crumbed topping. They are then thawed, topped and reheated, or just made in advance on the day, topped with crumbs and then popped in the oven for 20 minutes to warm through.

Ingredients

8oz Cod or other white fish
2oz bacon chopped
1 medium onion chopped
$^1/_2$ tsp chopped parsley
4 scallop shell shape dishes

$^1/_2$ pint milk
2oz butter
1oz flour
salt and pepper to taste

Method

1. Gently poach fish in the milk until cooked, (about 15 minutes), reserve milk for the sauce.
2. Chop onion and bacon.
3. Melt half of the butter, add the onions and bacon and cook gently until onion is softened but not browned.
4. Melt the remaining butter, make a roux sauce with the flour, adding the milk from the poached fish gradually, bring to the boil until it thickens.
5. Remove from the heat and add the parsley and seasoning and beat well.
6. Divide the cooked fish between the four scallop shells dishes, spoon over the bacon and onion mixture and the sauce. Cover with cling film and freeze.

Topping
Toast some white breadcrumbs and cover fish dish. Half way through the reheating, add tomato slices Return to the oven to finish off.   Oven 190C.

Margaret Wright, Dunchurch

Crab

Baked Eggs with Crab

Serves 4 - Time 25 minutes

Ingredients

Butter for greasing
175gms(6oz) tin of crabmeat
4 tsp brandy
4 large eggs
Salt and pepper
Cayenne pepper
Sprigs of chervil or parsley for garnish.

To serve Toast brown or white bread

Method

1. Pre-heat oven to 190C (375F) Gas mark 5. Lightly grease 4 ramekins with butter.

2. Place $\frac{1}{4}$ of the crabmeat in the bottom of the dishes, sprinkle the brandy over each.

3. Break an egg into each dish centrally, season with salt and pepper (and a spoonful of cream around the yolk optional). Sprinkle a spoonful of milk around the yolk and dust with cayenne.

4. Place dishes on baking tray and place in oven for 10-15 minutes for the whites to set.

Serve sprinkled with parsley and triangles of toast.

Stella Castle, Bideford

Crab and Noodle Soup

Ingredients

50 g (2oz) thin rice noodle
100 g (4oz) Chinese style stir-fry mix vegetables
2 tsp fish sauce
2 tsp sweet chilli sauce
600ml (1 pint) vegetable or fish stock
170g can of crabmeat
Handful fresh coriander leaves for garnish

Method

1. Put noodles and vegetables in a bowl and cover with boiling water, leave to soak about 5minutes to soften.

2. Heat together fish sauce, chilli sauce and stock in a pan.

3. Drain vegetables and noodles, divide between 2 bowls, adding the crabmeat.

4. Pour over the hot stock, scatter coriander leaves to garnish and serve.

Stella Castle, Bideford

Prawns

Prawn stuffed courgettes

Ingredients

4 courgettes
6oz (150g) peeled prawns
1 hard boiled egg chopped
$^1/_2$ pint (300ml) white sauce
1 tbsp grated parmesan

Oven temperature 180C/ 350F/ Gas 4

Method

Cut a small slice lengthways along the courgettes, scoop out the centre to form a cavity, chop finely and, blanch for 2 minutes in boiling salted water.
To the white sauce add the prawns, chopped egg and finely chopped courgette from the centre.
Fill the courgettes with this mixture and sprinkle on the parmesan cheese. Bake in oven for 15-20 minutes.
This filling can also be used for pastry cases or peppers.

Eleanor Bradshaw, Warwickshire

Prawn Chop Suey

Ingredients

6-8oz prawns (shelled)
4 tbsp oil
1 large onion sliced
1 large pepper (core and seeds removed, flesh shredded)
1 large carrot shredded
2 sticks celery sliced
1 tin (8oz) bean sprouts

For Topping
1 large egg   1 tbsp oil   salt and pepper

Method

Heat 3 tbsp oil in large frying pan and add onion, pepper, carrot and celery.
Shake pan over moderate heat until vegetables are barely cooked, add
prawns and drained bean sprouts, forking them well. Turn mixture into
round dish for serving.

Wipe out pan and reheat with remaining tbsp of oil.
To prepare topping: beat egg with oil season, and pour into the pan. Cook
gently until egg is set. Turn it with a slice and cook for a further ? minute.
Slide topping on to prawn chop suey and serve hot.

Jean Horncastle, Paignton

Hot Spicy Prawns with Campenella

Ingredients

225/8ozs tiger prawns, cooked and peeled.
1-2 garlic cloves, crushed.
Finely grated rind of 1 lemon
15mls / 1 tbsp lemon juice
1.5ml / $^1/_4$ tsp red chilli paste or large pinch chilli powder
15ml / 1 tbsp light soy sauce
150g / 5oz bacon rashers cut into strips/batons
1 shallot or smoked onion finely chopped
15ml / 1tbsp olive oil
225g / 8oz Campenella or other pasta shapes
60ml / 4 tbsp fish or vegetable stock
400g tin chopped tomatoes
2tbsp chopped fresh parsley seasoning

Method

Marinade the prawns in lemon juice mixed with soy sauce, garlic, lemon rind, chilli and seasoning. Leave for 1 hour.

Fry the shallots and bacon in oil. Add the tin of tomatoes and the stock, simmer gently until thickened. Place to one side.
Meanwhile cook pasta according to packet instructions, keep warm after straining into separate serving dish and mix in parsley.
Just before serving, drain the liquid from the marinade into the pan with the tomatoes and bring back to simmering point. At the last moment add in the prawns and return to simmering point.
When fully reheated (be careful not to overcook the prawns) put prawns into second separate bowl and serve.

Mrs R Hobson, Wells, Somerset

Knitted Christmas Tree at Atlantic Village, Bideford, winter 2005 © Alison Murray

The Knitted Gingerbread House, Bangkok 2009 © Alison Murray

Teaching, Bangkok 2009 © Alison Murray

W. Yorkshire Playhouse Heydays Knitters contribution © Alison Murray

Bags of Fish © Alison Murray

Appledore Scuba Club Knitting under the sea © James Wright

Diver from Jill Lewis © Alison Murray

Blue Coral © Alison Murray

31

Coral from Heather Harris © Alison Murray

Work on sea and cliffs in progress © Alison Murray

Sewing the inside walls © Alison Murray

Knitting on large needles © Alison Murray

R.N.L.I. Display © Alison Murray

Salmon

Salmon with a Cheesy Crunchy Crust

Ingredients

2 salmon fillets
1oz butter
2tbsp flaked almonds
2tbsp of chopped parsley
1oz Gruyere or Emmental cheese coarsely grated

Method

Pre-heat oven to 190C, 375F, Gas mark5

Season fillets.
Butter an ovenproof dish of suitable size and smear salmon with remaining butter
Mix cheese, parsley and almonds together and press on top of salmon
Bake for 15-20 minutes until topping is crisp and golden
Serve with new potatoes and green salad or broccoli

Margo Western, Huddersfield

Seafood Lasagne

To make 4 generous portions (can stretch to5/6 for a dinner party)
Note: Most ingredients ex Waitrose (tend to be the best) but
Tesco/Sainsbury will have the items as well.

Ingredients

Dry lasagna sheets x one pack (you'll only need half at most)
Lobster Bisque Tins (400g) x2 (Spinnaker is the best brand)
Raw seafood (can be frozen) x500g (personal choice)
(200g salmon, 150g scallops, 150g prawns)
Fresh spinach leaves x one pack
Strong cheddar cheese x300g

Method

Grate cheese and set aside in fridge.
Cook spinach very quickly (sauté in pan or cook in microwave in bag),
immediately chill in cold water, drain set aside in fridge.
Defrost seafood and drain, don't squeeze out excess liquid.
Cut the salmon fillet into small pieces.
Soak pasta sheets in cold water for 2/3 minutes
Take a suitable ovenproof dish and coat with a little olive oil.
Place a layer of pasta sheets in dish (break sheets to fit)
Coat with a little of the soup and 1/3rd of the mixed seafood
Top with 1/3rd of the spinach and then ? of the soup, followed by a
sprinkling of 50g of the cheese.
Repeat twice more until fish is used and you have a top layer of pasta.
Coat entire dish with remaining soup and cover with foil.
Leave to stand for 30 minutes to 2 hours.
Then cook for 40 minutes in middle of oven 170C, 325f, Gas mark 3.
Remove foil and top with the remaining cheese
Return to the oven for 15/20 minutes until golden brown.

Note: Better to place the dish on an ovenproof tray in case it bubbles over.

Good luck and enjoy

Roma Stephenson, Hampshire

Salmon Layer Betty

Ingredients

Crumb Mixture
6oz bread crumbs
3oz butter
Salt and pepper

Salmon Filling
Medium sized tin pink or red salmon
1oz butter
1oz flour
$^1/_2$ pint milk
Juice of lemon
1 egg yolk
$^1/_4$ peeled cucumber (chopped)
Seasoning, parsley to garnish

Method

1. Fry the breadcrumbs in butter until golden brown, season lightly.
2. Drain and flake the salmon.
3. Melt butter in a large saucepan add flour, cook for a few minutes without browning, remove from heat and gradually add the milk. Return to the heat, bring to the boil and allow sauce to thicken, stirring continuously. Remove from heat.
4. Add lemon juice and beat in egg yolk and add salmon.
5. Heat for another 2 minutes without boiling, add chopped cucumber and seasoning.
6. Arrange layers of salmon mixture and breadcrumbs alternately in an ovenproof dish, finishing off with a layer of breadcrumbs.
7. Bake in oven on a moderate heat until golden brown.
8. Garnish top with parsley when cooled.

Ivy Voysey, Somerset

Smoked Fish

Smoked Haddock Fishcakes

Ingredients

2lbs potatoes , peeled and cut into pieces
1lb smoked haddock fillet
6 tbsp tinned sweet corn
2 tbsp fresh parsley chopped
2 tsp finely grated lemon rind
2 tbsp seasoned flour
1 large egg beaten
3 oz fresh breadcrumbs

Method

Boil potatoes until cooked, drain and mash set aside to cool.

Place haddock in a pan cover with water and simmer gently for 8-10 minutes until cooked. Remove and flake the fish, discarding any bones or skin.

Add the flaked fish, sweet corn, parsley, chives and grated lemon rind to the mashed potatoes, season with salt and pepper and mix well.

Divide the mixture into eight fishcakes. Coat each with seasoned flour, dip in the beaten egg and coat with the breadcrumbs. Place in the fridge to chill for at least 30minutes.

Heat some oil in a frying pan. When hot, add the fishcakes and fry on each side for 3-4 minutes until golden brown. Carefully remove, drain and serve with salad and lemon wedges.

Pat Hindson, N. Devon

Creamy Haddock Bake

Ingredients

$^3/_4$ lb natural smoked haddock
3 medium sized potatoes
Bread crumbs
Poach the haddock for approximately 15 minutes, flake it by hand, making sure to remove al the bones, set aside for a while.

For the Sauce
$^3/_4$ oz plain flour
$^3/_4$ oz butter
$^1/_4$ tsp dry mustard
1 tsp parsley
4oz cheddar cheese
$^1/_2$ pint full cream milk
Pepper to taste

Method

Making the sauce
Put all the ingredients into a small saucepan (except for the cheese and milk)
Over a low heat, blend all the ingredients together until it forms a ball.
Slowly add the milk stirring continuously to prevent lumps. When the milk is blended in, cook gently for 2 minutes stirring as before. Remove pan from the heat and stir in 2oz of the cheese.
Stir the cooked haddock into the sauce, place in an ovenproof dish. Top with mashed potatoes and rest of the cheese and breadcrumbs.
Bake in the oven at Gas mark 4 for about 20 minutes or until top is nicely browned. Serve with vegetables of your choice.

EAT AND ENJOY.

Smoked Fish and Potato Pate

Serves 4

Ingredients

650g floury potatoes diced
300g smoked mackerel, skinned and flaked
75g cooked gooseberries
2 tsp lemon juice
2 tbsp crème fraiche
1 tbsp capers
1 gherkin chopped
1 tbsp chopped dill pickle
1 tbsp chopped fresh dill, salt and pepper
Lemon wedges to garnish

Method

1. Cook the diced potatoes in boiling water for 10 minutes until tender, drain well. Place the cooked potatoes in a food processor or blender.
2. Add the skinned and flaked mackerel and process for 30 seconds until fairly smooth, alternatively mash with a fork.
3. Add the cooked gooseberries, lemon juice and crème fraiche and blend for a further 10 seconds, or mash well.
4. Stir in the capers, gherkins, dill pickle and chopped fresh dill, Season with salt and pepper.
5. Turn the pate into a serving dish, garnish with lemon wedges. Serve with slices of toast or warm crusty bread.

Use stewed apples if gooseberries are unavailable.

Pat Hindson, N. Devon

Scallops

Baked Scallops

Ingredients

6 large scallops
1oz butter melted
Salt and pepper
Lemon juice
5 tbsp double cream
2 rounded tbsp fresh white breadcrumbs
4 bacon rashers (optional)

Method

Set oven at 375 F or Gas mark 5
Remove scallops from their shells wash and dry well. Put 1 tsp of melted butter on the bottom of each of the 4 shells.
Quarter the scallops and arrange in each of the shells, season and add a squeeze of lemon juice. Spoon over the cream; sprinkle the breadcrumbs over the scallops adding the rest of the melted butter.
Bake in the pre-heated oven for 8-10 minutes until golden brown.
The tops may be garnished with a curl of grilled bacon.

Jean Davie, Salcombe

Granny Crang's Sunday Scallops

Poach whole scallops including orange foot (feeler) until cooked, cool.

When cold place in dish and cover with malt vinegar overnight.

Eat with fresh brown bread and butter, sprinkle scallops with pepper if required, very tasty.

My gran used to do this dish as a simple tasty Sunday "tea", we used to have a "roast dinner" at lunchtime in the good old fashioned way, "lunch" was something posh people had!

Mavis Bewsher, Crediton

Trout

Fishy Parcels

Ingredients

1 Trout per person or salmon fillet per person
Margarine or Butter....1/2 per parcel
Mushrooms diced 1oz per person
Parsley chopped
Chives sliced
Lemon juice or lime juice
Black pepper

Method

Place each fillet on an oblong of foil
(enough foil to be able to create a parcel)
Divide mushrooms evenly between the fish
Sprinkle on the herbs, add butter/margerine
Add a squeeze of chosen juice
A little black pepper to taste

Fold foil to seal in all ingredients
Place in a warm oven 200, 400F, Gas mark 6
Or steam or barbecue
For approximately 20 minutes

Delicious! Serve with seasonal veggies or salad and crisp bread and a glass of bubbly!

Sally Jubb, Wareham, Dorset

Trout in Cider

Choose a trout with pink flesh (that is one which has been feeding on shrimp). Clean the trout and soak it overnight in cider (any variety). In the morning grill with butter and serve with mushrooms.

Another way to cook Trout or Salmon

For cold Salmon

Cover a piece of silver foil with olive oil and sprinkle with salt and pepper. Place fish or piece of fish in the foil and seal. Place dish in oven at 290F. A piece weighing 2lbs will be cooked in one hour. Leave it in foil to cool.

 For hot Salmon

The method is the same as the above except that butter is substituted for olive oil. When the fish is cooked, slide it straight out of the foil together with the juices.

Jean Horncastle, Paignton

Stuffed Trout

Clean and de-head trout
(Better still get the fishmonger to do this for you!)
Stuff with green pesto and pine nuts
Coat with olive oil
Sprinkle pine nuts on top.
Bake in a moderate oven for 25minutes.

Serve with your choice of fresh vegetables and mushrooms.

Joyce Curtis, Sleaford Lincolnshire

Fried Trout with Almonds

Serves 4

Ingredients

4 trout cleaned with the heads left on.
2 level tbsp flour seasoned with salt and pepper
4oz (100g) butter
1dsp olive oil
2 to 3 oz (50 to 75g) flaked almonds
Juice of $^1/_2$ lemon

Method

1. Wash and dry trout, dust lightly with seasoned flour

2. Heat 2oz (50g) butter and oil in frying pan, add trout 2 at a time and fry for 10 minutes turning once.

3. Drain well on soft kitchen paper and keep hot.

4. Wipe pan clean with soft kitchen paper, add rest of the butter and almonds and fry gently until the butter begins to turn golden brown.

5. Remove from heat and add lemon juice.

6. Pour over trout and serve straight away.

Delicious!!

Carol Halliday, Birmingham

Sprats

Sprat Pate

Using grilled sprats, which have been headed and boned. Mince up with lemon juice, pepper, fromage frais, cottage cheese and butter. Mix well together. Can be frozen.

Fish Bake

Grilled sprats, headed and boned, minced with mashed potatoes and seasoning. Then the mixture can be made into shapes, dipped in beaten egg then breadcrumbs, and either baked or grilled.

Fried Sprats

Baste sprats well in flour and fry in hot oil. Serve when golden brown with a slice of lemon.

Grilled Sprats

Grill for about six minutes on either side, then serve when golden brown.

Bernadette Richardson, Kirkham, Preston

Other Dishes & Stories

Thoughts of an Old Salt

When people decide to go sailing
To make the boat go it takes two
One to look after the sails and steer
The other looks after the crew

When the boats brand new and the weather
Is clear and you're not in a race
You can sit back, relax and not worry
For your boat has got plenty of space

But keep your eyes open for storm clouds
They're never very far away
Both captain and crew must be lookouts
Lest your boat begins to lose way

And if you find yourself in bad weather
Then remember it always takes two
Working together, with no-one in charge
If you're going to come out in the blue

If the boat is filled with life's treasures
There's more need for the crew to come good
It's no problem if both sit and remember
Once the boat was built of good wood

A boat deserves effort from crewmen
Perhaps more than the crewmen expects
But it's due to this lack of effort
That the sea is full of shipwrecks

J E Campbell Rayleigh

Kipper Pate

Ingredients

8oz kipper fillets with butter
1/2 clove garlic chopped
Fresh ground black pepper

8oz cream cheese
1 tbsp lemon juice
Pinch cayenne pepper

Method

Cook the kippers as directed on the packet. Drain and allow to cool
slightly. Remove the skin and mash the flesh to a pulp. Beat in the cream
cheese; add the garlic lemon juice and pepper to taste. Spoon the pate into
a serving dish or individual dishes and smooth the tops. Refrigerate for
about 1 hour before serving with toast cut into quarters and garnished with
lemon twists.

For a smoother texture put the cooked fish with all the other ingredients
into a blender and mix to desired consistency.

Anne-Marie, Caine, Exeter

Moules a la marinere

Soften a chopped onion and a clove of garlic in 1oz of butter.
Pour in half a bottle of dry white wine, then add 1 kilo of mussels washed
and scrubbed.
Cover with a lid and cook on a high heat for 4-5 minutes.
Remove from the heat and strain mussels into a bowl discarding any which
have not opened.
Reduce the liquid and add 3 tbsp of double cream and some freshly milled
black pepper and a little sea salt. Pour over the mussels and sprinkle a
tablespoon of chopped parsley over it.
Serve straight away with crusty French bread.

J H Strickland, Christchurch, Dorset

Monkfish Ricata with Courgette noodles

Serves 4

175 g (6oz) each of green and yellow courgettes topped and tailed. Cut with a mandoline into long strips resembling thin noodles, discarding central core of seeds.

20x25g (1oz) small slices of monkfish, salt and freshly ground black pepper, plain flour. Season fish with salt and pepper, dip into flour and shake of surplus.

1 large egg.
1 packet of saffron.
Beat together and then dip the slices into this.

30ml(2 tbsp) olive oil
Heat in a non stick pan, fry the fish for 2-3 minutes on each side until cooked and golden brown in colour. Keep warm.

Tomato concasse 275g (10 oz) tomatoes 1 large sprig thyme
Nick the skins of each tomato immerse in boiling for 10 seconds, remove and peel of the skins and halve the tomatoes. Remove the seeds using a teaspoon then chop the flesh very finely.

Heat the tomato and thyme gently together; add the courgette 'noodles' and season to taste with salt and pepper. Heat for 2-3 minutes, and then discard the thyme.

Arrange the courgette 'noodles' and tomatoes on individual plates, and then place the monkfish on top. Serve immediately.

Lizzie Breese, Rosemoor

Baked Oysters with Bacon

Ingredients

12 oysters removed from shell
12 rashers of streaky bacon

Method

Stretch out the bacon, roll the oysters in the bacon and secure with a cocktail stick.

Grill under a hot grill until the bacon is crisp and oysters are lightly cooked through.
Serve as a cocktail nibble.

Mair Lewis, Flintshire

Pilchard quiche

Ingredients

1 large tin if pilchards in tomato sauce
Shortcrust or puff pastry
2 large eggs   salt and pepper
1 large tomato to decorate the top

Method

Line a flan dish with the pastry.
Empty tin of pilchards into a bowl and remove bones etc. Mash together with the eggs, season and put into the pastry and cook at 200C, Gas mark 6 for 30 minutes.

Eileen Heasman, Crowborough, Sussex

Tuna Plait

Ingredients

8oz flaky pastry
2oz button mushrooms sliced
$^1/_2$ red pepper deseeded and sliced
1 egg beaten
Milk to glaze
1oz grated cheese
7oz can tuna in brine
2oz chopped onion
$^1/_2$ tsp oregano
1 tbsp vegetable stock   Set oven to Gas mark7 220C

Method

Drain and flake tuna into a bowl, stir in onion, red pepper, mushrooms and oregano, bind with beaten egg.
Add stock and sprinkle with black pepper to taste.

Roll out pastry 10"x8 x $^1/_4$" thick, place tuna mix down centre of pastry leaving $^1/_2$" each end to fold up and 2" at the sides.

Make diagonal cut down each side, brush pastry with water, bring up both ends and side strips alternately to make plait.

Roll out pastry trimmings into long strip and twist and place along top in centre. Brush with milk and sprinkle cheese across top.

Beryl Billings, Shropshire

Batter

Flour, water, baking powder
Mix to paste,
Add 2 tbsp of vinegar

Use at once!

Mrs Casemore, Barnstaple

Devon Flats Biscuits

Makes about 24

Ingredients

225g (8oz) SR Flour
Pinch of salt
100g (4oz) castor sugar
100ml (4floz) clotted or double cream
1 egg beaten
15ml (1 tbsp) fresh milk

Method

Mix the flour, salt and sugar together, stir in the cream, egg and enough milk to make a stiff dough.

Roll the dough on a lightly floured surface until about 0.75 (1/3inch) thick. Cut out circles using a 7.5cm (3inch) cutter.

Transfer to a greased baking sheet and bake at 220C, 425F, Gas mark 7 for about 8-10 minutes until light golden brown.

Transfer to wire racks to cool.

Pat Hindson, N. Devon

Helicopter trip

Whilst in the W.R.N.S. back in the 1950's I was stationed at H.M.S. Culdrose in Cornwall. Some early morning out to sea trips by helicopter pilots, consisted of them being able to lower nets down to local fisherman who popped in some freshly caught mackerel. Occasionally on these flights one was able to obtain an unofficial free ride. Needless to say I was one of these culprits so to speak.

This was my first flight ever in anything so I was very excited. Having done the necessary fishy part we were on our way back to the airfield when the Co-pilot told me not to panic but we had caught fire. The next thing I knew we just went down very fast but fortunately for all of us, believe it or not, landed in a pig field, which was very wet and soggy.

The helicopter I believe was a write-off and I was up before the First Officer. None of us were injured and I only got reprimanded and told next time I flew to make sure I had a flying chit. I never did find out what happened to the officers.

Thank goodness we didn't land in the sea, because although I had on a may west I'd been given on how to use it. It's as well things are much stricter today.

Mrs M Harris, Sussex

Bill the fisherman © Alison Murray

Granny on the beach © Alison Murray

Punch and Judy © Mike Lester

Beach Scene © Alison Murray

61

Beach and Sea © Alison Murray

Nemesis from Bradworthy Junior School, Devon © Alison Murray

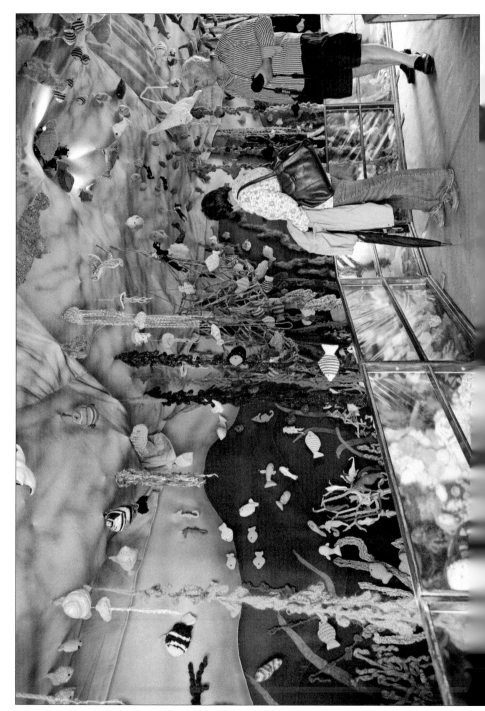

Under the Sea © Mike Lester

Undersea Creatures © Alison Murray

Fishermens Corner © Alison Murray

Appledore Lifeboat, The Molly Hunt © Mike Lester

Fish Provencal

Ingredients

3 fish fingers per person
1 small onion
2 tomatoes quartered
$^1/_2$ pepper diced
$^1/_2$ piece courgette diced

Method

Put the fish fingers in the bottom of a casserole and put the rest of the ingredients on top. Cover and place in the oven at 180deg C for 30 mins. Serve with either rice, pasta or oven chips.

Sue Leeder, Devon

Quick Tuna Pasta

Ingredients

120gms pasta
Small tin chick peas
Small tin red kidney beans
Small tin sweet corn
Small tin tuna
2 table spoons mayonnaise

Method

Cook the pasta, drain the beans, peas, sweet corn and tuna. Drain the pasta when cooked and mix with the rest of the ingredients. Serve

The mix of peas, beans etc. can be any tinned, cooked or frozen vegetable of choice.

Sue Leeder, Devon

The Loan Shark

I'll tell you a tale of the billowing blue
It's not very long and completely untrue

Sid was a squid with a problem one day
He'd travelled from home, a long distance away

And now he'd gone down with the maritime flu
Oh, what was our feverish mollusc to do?

He had to get home but he just couldn't swim
Perhaps someone kind would take pity on him?

He thought he would hitchhike and so put out
A tentative tentacle, waving about

Ted was a tuna a trustworthy fish
He saw Sidney's plight and granted his wish

"I'll give you a lift mate, just hang on to me"
And off the two sped through the depths of the sea

Sid was so grateful he clung on to Ted
And dozed as they covered the miles of seabed

But when he awoke it gave him a shock
They'd stopped at a large, unfamiliar rock

"Where are we?" asked Sid, "This is not the right way"
"A detour "said Ted, "I have debts I must pay"

"Mark!" he called out "Are you in there? It's Ted"
And out from a cavern appeared a grey head

The head was attached to a very large shark,
Evil of eye, and by name, Murky Mark,

"Morning there Fred, nice to see you old mate"!
Brought me a payment to cross off the slate?"

"I know it's been ages, my payments are slow
But finally here's the sick squid that I owe"

And that is the end of my pitiful song,
Completely untrue and not very long.

(Note for foreign readers: quid is English slang for pounds)

68

And Finally

How to make Amblouguss Pie

Take 4 pounds of fresh amblougusses and put them in a small pipkin.
Cover with water and boil them incessantly for 8 hours. Add 2 pints of
new milk and boil for another 4 hours.

When the amblougusses are quite soft, take them out and place in a wide
pan. Grate some nutmeg over them, cover with powdered gingerbread, curry
powder and a quantity of cayenne pepper.

Take the pan into the next room and place it on the floor. Bring it back
again and let it simmer for $3/4$ hour. Shake the pan violently till all the
amblougusses have become a pale purple colour.
Prepare a paste and insert the whole very carefully, adding a small pigeon,
2 slices of beef, 4 cauliflowers and any number of oysters. Watch patiently
till the crust begins to rise, adding a pinch of salt from time to time.

Serve up in a clean dish, and throw the whole lot out of the window as fast
as possible!!

Jean Horncastle, Paignton

Patterns

Little Mermaid Pattern

Front/Back same.

Tail   Cast on 15sts
Row 1 Rib K1 P1
Row 2 Rib
Row 3 K2tog Rib K2tog (13)
Row 4 Rib
Row 5 K2tog Rib K2tog (11)
Row 6 Rib
Row 7 K2tog Rib K2tog (9)
Row 8 Rib
Row 9 Change to Stocking Stitch (1 RowK 1 RowP)
Rows 10 - 12 Stocking Stitch
Row 13 Inc. 1st each end (11) continue in S.S.
Row 14 S.S.
Row 15 Inc. 1st each end (13)
Continue in S.S. until work measures 6", end with a purl row.

Body   Change to body colour, work 8 Rows end Purl
Next Row cast on 9sts K to end (22)
Next Row cast on 9sts K to end (31)
Work 2 Rows
Next Row Cast off 12sts K to end (19)
Next Row Cast off 12sts P to end (7)
Next Row K2tog K3 K2tog (5)

Head   Increase 1st each end of next 4 Rows (13)
Work 3 Rows
Next Row Decrease 1st each end & every Row until 3 remain.
Cast off.

Make Up Stitch front & Back sections together leaving end of tail open. Turn out & stuff. Finally sew up end of tail, embroider eyes & sew on hair.

Ann Murray

Spiral Shell

Cast on 6st sts leaving at least 8" yarn free

Row 1   P
Row 2   K1 (K into front and back of next st) 4 times, K1 (10sts)
Row 3   P
Row4   K1 (K into front and back of next st) 8 times, K1 (18sts)
Row 5   P
Row6   K1 (K into front and back of next st. K1) 8 times, K1 (26sts)
Row7   P
Row 8   K
Row 9   P
Row10   K1, s1, K1, psso, K to last 3 sts, K2tog, K1
Row11   P

Repeat until 4 stitches remain, break of yarn leaving at least 12" free and thread it through these 4 stitches.

Sew long sides together with an invisible seam, stuffing lightly as you go. Close up the bottom. It now looks like a carrot.

With both ends of the yarn together in the needle, secure with two or three small stitches at the edge of the bottom of the cone. Now make a spiral running stitch, picking up just a thread of the fabric every ? " and pulling the threads tight every half turn or so. You will see this gathers the cone up into a spiral. At the top, secure the gathering threads again with two or three small stitches and then hide them inside the stuffing.

Bridget Bythway

Limpet

Cast on 33 sts
Row 1   K1, P1 rib
Row 2   P1, K1 rib
Row 3   P1, (s1, K1, psso, K1, P1) to end (25sts)
Row 4   K1 (P2, K1) to end
Row 5   P1 (K2tog, P1) to end (17sts)
Row 6   P
Row 7   K1 (K2tog, P1) to end (9sts)
Row 8   P
Row 9   (K2tog) 4 times, K1 (5sts)

Break off yarn and thread through the 5 stitches. Sew up the side seam, stuff lightly and sew an oval of felt in the bottom.

Bridget Bythway

Starfish

Knitted in two pieces (front & back), No.4 needles, Double knitting wool (any colour)

Front –   Knitted in Stocking stitch (1 Row Plain, 1 Row Purl)
             **Cast on 4sts
             Next Row increase to 5 sts
             Then work 10 Rows
             Next Row increase to 7 sts
             Work 2 Rows more
             Leave sts on needle
             Repeat again from ** until you have 5 separate pieces on needle
             Join all 5 pcs together in one Row
             Work 2 Rows
             Next Row(Knit 2 tog K1) to end of Row
             Next Row K2 tog to end
             Continue until 2 sts remain, cast off

Back –   Knit in Garter st (every Row K)
             Work to same shapings
             Sew together and stuff

Alison Murray

Crochet Coral

Foundation ring: using double knitting wool and a 4.00mm crochet hook make 5ch.ss into last chain to form a ring.

Round 1;3 ch (counts as first tr) 14 trs into ring

Round 2: 3ch (counts as first tr) 2 trs into next st, (3tr into next stitch to end)ss into top of 3rd chain

Round 3; as round 2 fasten off.

To make a larger size repeat round 2 as many times as required

Fish

Make 2 pieces the same.
 Knitting needles – 1 pair $3^1/4$mm (UK10 - USA3)
Using A (main colour) cast on 13 sts.
Ist Row (Right Side). - Knit
2nd Row. - P1, *k1, p1; rep from * to end.
These 2 rows form the pattern. Keeping pattern correct dec 1 st at each end of next and following 2 alt rows. 7 sts remain. Work 1 row.
Keeping pattern correct and working in stripes of 2 rows in B (contrast colour) and 2 rows in A, inc 1 st at each end of next and every alt row until there are 17 sts.
Work 5 rows straight, thus ending with 2 rows in B.
Keeping stripes correct dec1 st at each end of next and following alt row. 13 sts remain.
Work 1 row. Break off B and using A only continue to dec 1 st at each end of next and every alt row until 5 sts remain. Cast off.

To make up.

Using Black embroider eye on each piece.. Sew 2 pieces together leaving a small opening. Stuff firmly and close opening.

The fish can be plain as well as stiped, sizes altered by using larger needles and thicker yarn

This Book is also dedicated to

Vera Fisher, Devon
Jenny Harrison, Cornwall
Steve Le Doux, Cornwall
Patience Honor Cartwright, Devon

Acknowledgments

We would like to thank everyone who has knitted, or contributed in any way to this project, because without all their hard work and generosity we could not have achieved such a fantastic result.

Special thanks to

Kingsley School, Bideford
John Pavitt Engineering, Bideford
Mike Jubb for 'Shark Attack'
Bryan Sentence for 'Mermaids'
James Wright, Appledore Sub-Aqua Club for photographs
Mike Lester (www.mikelesterphotography.co.uk)

Kindly sponsored by:

Arts Council England
Coldharbour Mill, Uffculme
Kingsley School, Bideford
John Pavitt Engineering, Bideford
The Big Sheep, Abbotsham
Bideford Van Hire & Self Storage Ltd

Knitters and helpers

Groups

1st Ottery St Mary Guides
Arun Valley Craft & Needlework Group
Barnes Friendly Craft Club, Sunderland
Bideford W.I.
Blackhill Methodist Church, Co. Durham
Bradworthy School, Devon
Bristol Steiner School
Brook Valley W.I., E. Sussex
Brunel Quilters, Cornwall
Bygate W.I. Craft Class, Northumberland
Byker Knitting & Craft Club, Newcastle upon Tyne
Chelsfield W.I. Afternoon Club
Chepstow Knitters
Combe Martin Craft Club, Devon
Cramlington Craft Club, Northumberland
Curdworth W.I. Warwickshire
Draveil Patchwork, France
Elm Rd (Beckenham W.I.)
Farningham W.I.
Gilbert Court Sheltered Housing Scheme
Hayes W.I. Kent
Helping Hands Knitting Group, Wales
Heydays, W. Yorks. Playhouse
Holbrook W.I. Gosport
Jenny Murray & Friends, Morpeth
Julie Clarks Textile Craft Group, U3A Harrogate
Krafty Tarts
Krafty Tarts Craft Club, Bristol
Leighton Buzzard Knitting & Crochet Guild
Looe Knit & Natter
Multi-ply Knitting Group, N Yorkshire
Norfolk Branch, Knitting & Crochet Guild

Knitters and helpers

Nutty Knitters of Yeo Vale Road, Devon
Oakdale Ward, Plympton Hospital
Otford Evening W.I. Craft Group, Kent
Over 60's Club, Shaldon
Penrith Craft Class
Ravenswood W.I.
Salcombe Lifeboat Guild
Saltash U3A Craft Group, Cornwall
Saltdean Oval Knit & Natter Group
Selston Knitting & Craft Club, Nottinghamshire
Shaldon Over 60's Club
Shoreham W.I. Kent
St. Georges Beckenham W.I., Kent
St. Ives Knitting Club
St. Stephens Church Crafty Taskers Group, East Sussex
Stitch & Bitch, East Dulwich
Sussex Crafts Knitting Group
The Arcade Knitters, Littlehampton
The Big Sheep Knitting Club, Devon
The Church of Jesus Christ of Latter Day Saints (Exeter)
The Happy Knitters of Hurstpierpoint
The Jolly Stitchers, Northants
The Langton Craft Group, Lincs
Tyne & Wear Branch, Knitting & Crochet Guild
West Buckland W.I. Somerset
West Kingsdown W.I. Kent
West Oxford U3A
Whickham Fellside W.I., Newcastle upon Tyne

With apologies to anyone who we may have accidentally omitted or for any mis-spelt names or places.

Individuals

Ruth,   Devon
Brenda, Yeo Vale
Dot, Yeo Vale
Lillian, Yeo Vale
Little Joan, Yeo Vale
Mary, Yeo Vale
Rosemary, Yeo Vale

A
Gillian Ackland, Somerset
Carole Adams, Middx
Jane Adams, Tyne & Wear
Ann Ainsworth, Herts
Mrs Joyce M Akrill, Cardiff
Carol Allen,
Alia Allim, Cardiff
Mrs Margaret Anderson, Somerset
Sue Andrews, Devon
Kate Armfield, Devon
Jane Ashby, Kent
Mrs Jean Ashdown, Devon
Barbara Atkinson, Devon
Mrs Phyllis E Avant, Staffs
Mrs J.E. Ayres, Beds

B
Barbara Bailey, Somerset
Mrs Lilian Bailey, Devon
Margaret Ballantyne, Devon
Val Balman
Jacci Bamber
Judith Banks
Mrs Vivienne Barber, Devon
Mrs Elizabeth Barber, Warwickshire

Barbara Barber

Sylvia Barber

Vera Barker, Devon

Vera Banner, Devon

Elysha Barrit, Somerset

Suzanne Barritt, Devon

Jane Barton, Bedfordshire

Mrs Eveline Bayard, Devon

Ann Beaman, Warks

Mrs Janet Bennett

Mavis, Bewsher, Devon

Mrs M Bickerton, Buckinghamshire

Mrs Jean Bickett, Sunderland

Mrs Beryl Billings, Shropshire

Mrs Shirley Binder, Lancs

Jean Birkett, Sunderland

Jackie Bishop, Northamptonshire

Celia Blackmore, Wales

Jean Blake

Ann Blatchford

Barbara Blight, Devon

Pauline Blundell

Gladys Bonham, Northamptonshire

Rachel Bonnick, Devon

Cindy Boot, Suffolk

Mrs Sandra Booth (& Jessica), Derbyshire

Miss A Bound, W.Sussex

Sarah Bowden, Devon

Mrs Mary Bowden, Devon

Rosie Bowditch, Dorset

Mrs Elizabeth Bowler, Oxfordshire

Mrs V Box, W.Yorks

Eleanor Bradshaw, Warks

Jenny Bradshaw

Liz Brewer, Shropshire

Elizabeth Brewer, Shropshire

Mrs Laurie Brock, Tyne & Wear

Marion Brockett, Cambs

Margaret Brooks, Tyne & Wear

Jaz Brophy, Thailand

Marion Brown, Huddersfield

Jordan Bulled, Devon

George & Pat Bullen, Kent

Mrs Deborah Burns, Devon

Bridgt Bythway, Devon

C

Brooke Cable, Devon

Mrs Anne Caine, Devon

Rosalie I Campbell, Essex

Ann Carr

David Cartwright

S. Carruthers, Merseyside

Mrs Margaret Carver, West Yorks

Mrs Jude Casemore, Devon

Stella Castle, Devon

Janet Clark,

Mrs Sheila Clarke, Tyne & Wear

Mrs M J Cocks, W.Sussex

Mrs Margaret Coe, Monmouth

Mrs L Connett, Tyne & Wear

Mrs Beryl Convery, W. Midlands

Janet Cook, W.Midlands

Margaret Cook,

Mrs Helen Cooper, Northamptonshire

Mrs Sheila A Cooper, W.Midlands

Joan Cope, Berkshire

Debbie Corke, Dorset

Mrs Mary Course, Devon

Victoria Cranfield

Jacqueline Crettez, France

Thelma Crook, Devon

Margaret Crowther
Mrs Margaret Cuff, Devon
Ann Cull, Devon
Mrs Joyce Curtis, Lincolnshire
Alissa Cush, Devon

D

Anthea Davidson, Herts
Enid Davidson
Mrs Jean Davie, Devon
Brenda Davies
Molly Davies, Cornwall
Mrs Jean Davis, Devon
Mrs Jillian Dean, Essex
J Defrates, Wilts
Mrs J Dickie, Fife
Enid Dimmock
Margarita Dixon, North Lincs
Julia Docherty
Miss Angela Doel, Hants
Marie-Louise Doherty, Gt. Malvern
Rita Drummond
Mrs Betty Duce, Hants
Sue Duckworth, Glos
Rita Duemmel, Cornwall
Lydia Duemmel
Doreen Duncason, Tyne & Wear
Renee Durndell
Mrs E Durrant, Oxfordshire
Mrs C Dymond, Devon
Shirley Dyson, N.Yorkshire

E

Mrs Jane Edger, Mid Glamorgan
Gill Edwards, Hampshire
Mrs J Edwards, Leicestershire

Mrs Muriel Ellerby, Tyne & Wear
Ann Elliot, Tyne & Wear
Dee & Jim Ellis, Devon
Carole Elsey, W.Yorkshire
Jean & Lynn Epsly, Northumberland
Shirley Eveleigh, Sussex
Sheila Everard, Tyne & Wear

F

Peggy Fairburn
Mrs P Falmer, Leicestershire
Jan Farley, Devon
Mrs M Farmer, Wales
Pat Farrow, Staffs
Penny Finkin
Ishbel Finlayson, Aberdeenshire
Ann Finn, Surrey
Vera Fisher
Susan Flint, Leicestershire
Jay Foote, Cornwall
Jackie Ford
Christine Forder, Devon
Sue Forrest, Middx
Eleanor Freelove

G

Ann Galan-Huertas, Cornwall
Kay Gallacher
Anne Garrod, Herts
Mrs Linda Gates, Middx
Mary German
Sheila Gibson, W.Yorkshire
Mrs Rosemary Glanville, Devon
Mrs Muriel Gollop (& Sue), Somerset
Mrs Gould, Devon
Elsie Goward

Mrs Sylvia Granger, Wales
Mrs Linda Grant, Wellington
Mrs S Grant, Sunderland
Mrs Amanda Green, Leicestershire
Mrs M Green, Devon
Maureen Green, Essex
Marilyn Green, Avon
Marion Green, Bucks
Maureen Green, Essex
Mrs G Gregory, Surrey
Suzy Griffith, Cornwall
Margaret Guest, Devon
Alice Gwynne-Jones, Powys

H
Edna Haffield, Essex
Carol Halliday, W.Midlands
Maddy Hamilton, Kent
Mary Harper, Gloucestershire
Christine Harris, Devon
Mrs Val Harris, Wales
Mrs Margaret Harris, Sussex
Joshua Harris (age13)
Cameron Harris (age 9)
Godfrey Harrisson
Mrs W Harrison, S. Yorkshire
Mrs A R Hart, Devon
Pat & Emma Hartley, Kent
Mrs J Hartnoll, N.Devon
Ruby Hayes, Somerset
Bev Heard
Mrs A R Heel, Co.Durham
Mrs Doreen Hemsworth, Essex
Pauline Hennessey, Ireland
B Heywood, Devon
Rosemary M Hibson, Somerset

Liz Hickman, Devon
Pam Hicks, I.O.W.
June Higgins
Angie Hindson, Devon
Mandie Hindson, Surrey
Pat Hindson, Devon
Jenny Hobbs
Mary Hole, Devon
Marguerite Holland, N.Devon
Diane Holm, Lancs
Mrs Joyce Horlock, W.Bucks
Jean Horncastle, Devon
Angela Hoskins
Laurence Le Hoverou, France
Dorothy Howe, Co.Durham
Sandra Hughes, Merseyside
Linda Hunkin, Cornwall
Mrs Christina Hunter, Cambs
Janet Hynes

I
Mrs Sandra Irving, Tyne & Wear

J
Mrs Jean Jackman, Tyne & Wear
Judith Jackson, Northumberland
Mrs Liz Jennings, Devon
Mrs Anne Johnson, Cheshire
Mrs A Johnson, Somerset
Anne Jones, Wales
Barbara Jones, Powys
Helen Jordan, W.Yorkshire
Mrs Nita Jordan, Devon
Sally Jubb, Dorset

K

Margaret Karnes, W.Sussex

Mrs Brenda Keesing, Northumberland

Dee King

Shirley Knight, Oxfordshire

Sheena McDonald, Scotland

Joyce Knight, Dorset

L

Kath Lamb

Maria Lannon

Mrs J Lawrence

Mrs Sheila Lee, Wilts

Sue Leeder, Devon

Judy Leggett, Hants

Maureen Leggatt

Lynn Lenace, Cornwall

Jane Lewis, Herts

Jillian Lewis, Somerset

Mrs Mair Lewis, N.Wales

Michelle Lewis, Devon

Morgan Lewis, Devon

Mrs Angela Liddles, Lancs

Mrs V Lister, Somerset

Jackie Llewellyns, Devon

Mrs A Lock, Merseyside

Madeline Locke

Mrs C Lockhart, Northumberland

Connor Long (age 10)

Caitlin Long (age 4)

Daphne Lovelace, Devon

Mrs Sylvia Lovell, Devon

Gill Ludbrook, Somerset

Mrs Lure, Merseyside

Mrs S D Lyons, Kent

M

Mrs Heather MacMillan, Ross-Shire
Mrs Diane Makepiece, Tyne & Wear
Mrs Jeanette Mansell, Wilts
M A Marsden, Vale of Glamorgan
Mrs Caroll Martin, Essex
Mrs Maureen Martin, Devon
Rose Martin
Miss Betty Mathrick, Somerset
Mrs A Mattock
Mrs Kathleen McGill
Mrs V McGuck, Tyne & Wear
Norma McIntosh
Lucy McLeod (age9), Northumberland
Max McLeod (age 7), Northumberland
Dan McLeod (age3), Northumberland
Mary McMahon, Ireland
Meg McMahon, Ireland
Mary McManus, Ireland
Lily McManus, Ireland
M McQuade, Scotland
Dorothy McSkimming
Linda Merrick, Berkshire
Mrs Milan, Northumberland
Christine Miles, Somerset
Barbara Miles, Somerset
Sheena Millar
Mary J Millar
Mrs Valerie Miller, Tyne & Wear
Mrs M Miller, N.Yorkshire
D Millington, W.Midlands
Margaret Mills
Elizabeth Minogue, Ireland
Jean Montgomery, Slough
Mrs J Moorley, Cornwall
Charlotte Moosa, Devon

Mrs M Moy

Joan Murray, Northumberland

N

Miss L Need, W.Midlands

Mary Nelson

Jean Newson

Lindsey Norman, Hong Kong

Ruth Nugent

O

Rosemary O'Callaghan

Mrs Anne Olde, Devon

Mrs Judith Osborne, Warks

Mrs V Osborne, Staffs

Rosemary Osbourne, Devon

Sandra Oswick, Essex

P

Ann Painter, Oxon

Mrs Parker, Gloucester

Dawn Parker, Warwick

Hazel Parker

Mrs B Parker, Glos

Mrs Marion Parkman, S.Wales

Maureen Patmore, Devon

Mrs June Peace, Dorset

Deborah Peacock, Co.Durham

Mrs S Pearce

Mrs Megan Pearsall, Worcestershire

Milly Pearson

Audrey Pearson

Mrs Anne Pepper, Kent

Mrs Ann Perkins, Surrey

Margaret Perkins

Hazel Peterson

Iris Phillips, Middx

Mrs K Phillips, N.Wales

L Pidgeon, Devon

Bridget Pike, Devon

Pat Plant

Lynn Pockett, Gloucestershire

Wendy Poole, Bedfordshire

Willow Popple, Devon

Gwen Potter, Hants

Jenny Potts, Warks

Mrs Jean Preece, Devon

Mrs A Preston, Merseyside

Q

Mrs M Quantock, Devon

Gillian Quigley, Kent

R

Mrs Radcliffe, Somerset

Mrs Diana Rawston, Lancs

Mrs M Read, Leicestershire

Janet Reed, Devon

Yvonne Reeves

Mrs Jan Richardson, Selkirkshire

Bernadette Richardson, Lancs

Joan Rickards, Devon

Linda Rickfield, Kent

Rose Ridgeway, Cornwall

Pauline Roberts, N.Yorkshire

Myra Robertson, Fife

Catherine Robson, Lancs

Mary Robson, Tyne & Wear

Christine Rodgers, Dorset

Dorothy Roebuck, Huddersfield

Mrs Shirley Rookley, Devon

Gwen Roper, Essex

Shirley Routh, Cleveland
Mrs P Royce, Somerset
Myrtle A. Ruiz, Oxon
Mrs Dorothy Rumbles, Berkshire

S

Mrs Mary Sanderson, Co.Durham
Mrs Jennifer Sargent, Devon
Rev. & Mrs Satterly, N.Cornwall
Mrs Doreen Savage, Saltdean
Stella Savage, W.Sussex
Mrs Joan Sawyer
Mrs Phyllis Scott, Northumberland
Mrs G Seabrook, Kent
Mrs Rosemary Seaby, Devon
B.G. Setchell, W.Sussex
Mrs Margaret Shaddick, Devon
Mrs Sandra Shanks, Norfolk
Catherine Le Saout, France
Alan Le Saout, France
Cecile Le Saout, France
Netta Scattergood, Devon
Mrs Janet Shanks, Perthshire
Bev Sherbon, London
Clair & Margaret Sherriff, W.Sussex
Sue Shotter, Cornwall
Mrs R Siemmens
Kay Simms, Devon
Margaret Simpson
Helen Sims, Devon
Anne Skene
Anne Skinner, Devon
Jean Skinner
Elizabeth Slade, W.Yorkshire
Ann Smith, Devon
Mrs Eunice Smith, Wiltshire

Mrs T Smith
Mrs Wendy Smith, East Sussex
Jane Smith, E.Midlands
Diane Smith
Lisa Snowdon, Devon
Rita Soady
Joan Somerset, Kent
Ruth Souster
Hazel Spencer, Dorset
Mrs Rosa Spicer, Berkshire
Sylvia Spiller
June Stavrinaki, Cyprus
Zoe Stavrinaki, Cyprus
Christine Steadman
Bridget Steers, London
Brenda Stephenson, Devon
Dot Stevens, Devon
Mrs J Stevens, Devon
Lynn Stewart
Mrs J.H.Stickland, Dorset
Patricia M Stredwick, E.Sussex
Mrs Alice Swan, Herts

T
Clare Tadman
Alison Tamplin
Patricia Tanti, Essex
Mrs Pamela Tardo, Wales
A.M. Taylor, Devon
Mrs Maureen Taylor, W.Midlands
Hilary Thackray, W.Yorkshire
Angela Thames, Hants
Mrs Adele Thomas, Llanelli
Leslie Thompson, Wiltshire
Georgina Thompson, Wiltshire
Carole Ann Thorme, Spain

Jenny Thorpe, W.Sussex
Carol Thwaites, Sunderland
Anita Tovey & Family, W.Midlands
Elaine Townsend, E.Midlands
Josie Truscott, Glos
Mrs D.M. Trussell, Devon
Doris Trussell
Mrs Dorothy Turner, Devon
Helena Turner, Cornwall

V

Patricia Valentine, Yorkshire
Phillipa Vardiss
May Varney, Beds

W

Jo Wainwright, Surrey
Judith Ward, Somerset
Audrey Watt, Mid Glamorgan
Mrs A Wells, Devon
Grace Wells, Devon
Mrs Pat Welstead, Hants
Margo Weston, Huddersfield
Trudy Weston, Devon
Mrs Heather Whit, Berkshire
Mrs M.B. Willetts
Diane Williams, Kent
Ethel Williams
Joan Wood, Northants
Sandie Wood, Kent
Cathy Worley, Cornwall
Margaret Wright, Warwickshire
Lesley Wright, Dorset

Y

Jean M Yookin
Christine Young, Lincolnshire
Barbara Young, Northumberland
Viv Young, Devon
Mrs C.A. Young

Notes